This Steps for Goal Setting Workbook Belongs To:

_____

I am ready, willing and able to achieve all of my goals.

This workbook is divided into 52 weekly sections of three pages per week section.

➢ Pages 4-5 have space to write 26 goals for the year. (1 Goal for every 2 Weeks)
➢ Every 2 weeks write down a new goal on your weekly sections.
➢ Date each of the weeks to better track your progress.
➢ Pay attention to the "Steps I Can Take To Reach It" section so you can break your goals into smaller steps and reachable targets.

Breaking down your goals into actionable, measurable and small steps, that are time-based is part of what are called **S.M.A.R.T.** Goals

Join the Goal Achievers Community and get your **FREE goal training and resources**.

Go here to sign up:
https://YourSpiritualityMatters.com/Goals

Things I Want to Do This Year

Success and Accomplishment Begins With a Dream.

Write down 26 goals/hopes/dreams you have for this year. Every 2 weeks you will begin work on a new goal. Follow the instructions in the workbook to detail, manage, accomplish and track your goals. The resource site has a FREE training guide and videos to help you with your goals and the SMART Goal concept.
https://YourSpiritualityMatters.com/Goals

1._____

2. _____

3. _____

4. _____

5. _____

6. _____

7. _____

8. _____

9. _____

10._____

11. _____

12. _____

13. _____

14. _____

15. _____

16. _____

17. _____

18. _____

19. _____

20. _____

22. _____

23. _____

24. _____

25. _____

26. _____

Week 1

Main Goal For This Week

_____

_____

_____

Steps I Can Take to Reach It

1.

2.

3.

4.

5.

Reward if I Make Good Progress

_____

Obstacles I May Face	How I Will Deal With Them

Accountability Partner

Deadline to Finish

Random Thoughts

Random Thoughts

Week 2

Main Goal For This Week

Steps I Can Take to Reach It

6.

7.

8.

9.

10.

Reward if I Make Good Progress

Obstacles I May Face	How I Will Deal With Them

Accountability Partner

Deadline to Finish

Random Thoughts

Random Thoughts

Week 3

Main Goal For This Week

_____

_____

_____

_____

Steps I Can Take to Reach It

11.

12.

13.

14.

15.

Reward if I Make Good Progress

_____

_____

Obstacles I May Face	How I Will Deal With Them

Accountability Partner

Deadline to Finish

Random Thoughts

Random Thoughts

Week 4

Main Goal For This Week

_____

_____

_____

_____

Steps I Can Take to Reach It

16.

17.

18.

19.

20.

Reward if I Make Good Progress

_____

_____

Obstacles I May Face	How I Will Deal With Them

Accountability Partner

Deadline to Finish

Random Thoughts

Random Thoughts

Week 5

Main Goal For This Week

_____

_____

_____

Steps I Can Take to Reach It

21.

22.

23.

24.

25.

Reward if I Make Good Progress

_____

Obstacles I May Face	How I Will Deal With Them

Accountability Partner

_____

_____

Deadline to Finish

_____

_____

Random Thoughts

Random Thoughts

Week 6

Main Goal For This Week

_____

_____

_____

_____

Steps I Can Take to Reach It

26.

27.

28.

29.

30.

Reward if I Make Good Progress

_____

_____

Obstacles I May Face	How I Will Deal With Them

Accountability Partner

Deadline to Finish

Random Thoughts

Random Thoughts

Week 7

Main Goal For This Week

_____

_____

_____

_____

Steps I Can Take to Reach It

31.

32.

33.

34.

35.

Reward if I Make Good Progress

_____

_____

Obstacles I May Face	How I Will Deal With Them

Accountability Partner

Deadline to Finish

Random Thoughts

Random Thoughts

Week 8

Main Goal For This Week

Steps I Can Take to Reach It

36.

37.

38.

39.

40.

Reward if I Make Good Progress

Obstacles I May Face	How I Will Deal With Them

Accountability Partner

Deadline to Finish

Random Thoughts

Random Thoughts

Week 9

Main Goal For This Week

_____

_____

_____

_____

Steps I Can Take to Reach It

41.

42.

43.

44.

45.

Reward if I Make Good Progress

_____

_____

Obstacles I May Face	How I Will Deal With Them

Accountability Partner

Deadline to Finish

Random Thoughts

Random Thoughts

Week 10

Main Goal For This Week

_____

_____

_____

_____

Steps I Can Take to Reach It

46.

47.

48.

49.

50.

Reward if I Make Good Progress

_____

_____

Obstacles I May Face	How I Will Deal With Them

Accountability Partner

Deadline to Finish

Random Thoughts

Random Thoughts

Week 11

Main Goal For This Week

_____

_____

_____

_____

Steps I Can Take to Reach It

51.

52.

53.

54.

55.

Reward if I Make Good Progress

_____

_____

Obstacles I May Face	How I Will Deal With Them

Accountability Partner

Deadline to Finish

Random Thoughts

Random Thoughts

Week 12

Main Goal For This Week

_____

_____

_____

_____

Steps I Can Take to Reach It

56.

57.

58.

59.

60.

Reward if I Make Good Progress

_____

_____

Obstacles I May Face	How I Will Deal With Them

Accountability Partner

Deadline to Finish

Random Thoughts

Random Thoughts

Week 13

Main Goal For This Week

Steps I Can Take to Reach It

61.

62.

63.

64.

65.

Reward if I Make Good Progress

Obstacles I May Face	How I Will Deal With Them

Accountability Partner

Deadline to Finish

Random Thoughts

Random Thoughts

Week 14

Main Goal For This Week

_____

_____

_____

Steps I Can Take to Reach It

66.

67.

68.

69.

70.

Reward if I Make Good Progress

_____

_____

Obstacles I May Face	How I Will Deal With Them

Accountability Partner

Deadline to Finish

Random Thoughts

Random Thoughts

Week 15

Main Goal For This Week

_____

_____

_____

_____

Steps I Can Take to Reach It

71.

72.

73.

74.

75.

Reward if I Make Good Progress

_____

_____

Obstacles I May Face	How I Will Deal With Them

Accountability Partner

Deadline to Finish

Random Thoughts

Random Thoughts

Week 16

Main Goal For This Week

_____

_____

_____

_____

Steps I Can Take to Reach It

76.

77.

78.

79.

80.

Reward if I Make Good Progress

_____

_____

Obstacles I May Face	How I Will Deal With Them

Accountability Partner

Deadline to Finish

Random Thoughts

Random Thoughts

Week 17

Main Goal For This Week

_____

_____

_____

_____

Steps I Can Take to Reach It

81.

82.

83.

84.

85.

Reward if I Make Good Progress

_____

_____

Obstacles I May Face	How I Will Deal With Them

Accountability Partner

Deadline to Finish

Random Thoughts

Random Thoughts

Week 18

Main Goal For This Week

Steps I Can Take to Reach It

86.

87.

88.

89.

90.

Reward if I Make Good Progress

Obstacles I May Face	How I Will Deal With Them

Accountability Partner

Deadline to Finish

Random Thoughts

Random Thoughts

Week 19

Main Goal For This Week

Steps I Can Take to Reach It

91.

92.

93.

94.

95.

Reward if I Make Good Progress

Obstacles I May Face	How I Will Deal With Them

Accountability Partner

Deadline to Finish

Random Thoughts

Random Thoughts

Week 20

Main Goal For This Week

_____

_____

_____

_____

Steps I Can Take to Reach It

96.

97.

98.

99.

100.

Reward if I Make Good Progress

_____

_____

Obstacles I May Face	How I Will Deal With Them

Accountability Partner

Deadline to Finish

Random Thoughts

Random Thoughts

Week 21

Main Goal For This Week

_____

_____

_____

_____

Steps I Can Take to Reach It

101.

102.

103.

104.

105.

Reward if I Make Good Progress

_____

_____

Obstacles I May Face	How I Will Deal With Them

Accountability Partner

Deadline to Finish

Random Thoughts

Random Thoughts

Week 22

Main Goal For This Week

Steps I Can Take to Reach It

106.

107.

108.

109.

110.

Reward if I Make Good Progress

Obstacles I May Face	How I Will Deal With Them

Accountability Partner

Deadline to Finish

Random Thoughts

Random Thoughts

Week 23

Main Goal For This Week

Steps I Can Take to Reach It

111.

112.

113.

114.

115.

Reward if I Make Good Progress

Obstacles I May Face	How I Will Deal With Them

Accountability Partner

Deadline to Finish

Random Thoughts

Random Thoughts

Week 24

Main Goal For This Week

Steps I Can Take to Reach It

116.

117.

118.

119.

120.

Reward if I Make Good Progress

Obstacles I May Face	How I Will Deal With Them

Accountability Partner

Deadline to Finish

Random Thoughts

Random Thoughts

Week 25

Main Goal For This Week

_____

_____

Steps I Can Take to Reach It

121.

122.

123.

124.

125.

Reward if I Make Good Progress

_____

Obstacles I May Face	How I Will Deal With Them

Accountability Partner

Deadline to Finish

Random Thoughts

Random Thoughts

Week 26

Main Goal For This Week

Steps I Can Take to Reach It

126.

127.

128.

129.

130.

Reward if I Make Good Progress

Obstacles I May Face	How I Will Deal With Them

Accountability Partner

_____

_____

Deadline to Finish

_____

_____

Random Thoughts

Random Thoughts

Week 27

Main Goal For This Week

Steps I Can Take to Reach It

131.

132.

133.

134.

135.

Reward if I Make Good Progress

Obstacles I May Face	How I Will Deal With Them

Accountability Partner

Deadline to Finish

Random Thoughts

Random Thoughts

Week 28

Main Goal For This Week

Steps I Can Take to Reach It

136.

137.

138.

139.

140.

Reward if I Make Good Progress

Obstacles I May Face	How I Will Deal With Them

Accountability Partner

Deadline to Finish

Random Thoughts

Random Thoughts

Week 29

Main Goal For This Week

_____

_____

_____

_____

Steps I Can Take to Reach It

141.

142.

143.

144.

145.

Reward if I Make Good Progress

_____

_____

Obstacles I May Face	How I Will Deal With Them

Accountability Partner

Deadline to Finish

Random Thoughts

Random Thoughts

Week 30

Main Goal For This Week

Steps I Can Take to Reach It

146.

147.

148.

149.

150.

Reward if I Make Good Progress

Obstacles I May Face	How I Will Deal With Them

Accountability Partner

_____

_____

Deadline to Finish

_____

_____

Random Thoughts

Random Thoughts

Week 31

Main Goal For This Week

Steps I Can Take to Reach It

151.

152.

153.

154.

155.

Reward if I Make Good Progress

Obstacles I May Face	How I Will Deal With Them

Accountability Partner

Deadline to Finish

Random Thoughts

Random Thoughts

Week 32

Main Goal For This Week

Steps I Can Take to Reach It

156.

157.

158.

159.

160.

Reward if I Make Good Progress

Obstacles I May Face	How I Will Deal With Them

Accountability Partner

Deadline to Finish

Random Thoughts

Random Thoughts

Week 33

Main Goal For This Week

_____

_____

_____

_____

Steps I Can Take to Reach It

161.

162.

163.

164.

165.

Reward if I Make Good Progress

_____

_____

Obstacles I May Face	How I Will Deal With Them

Accountability Partner

Deadline to Finish

Random Thoughts

Random Thoughts

Week 34

Main Goal For This Week

Steps I Can Take to Reach It

166.

167.

168.

169.

170.

Reward if I Make Good Progress

Obstacles I May Face	How I Will Deal With Them

Accountability Partner

Deadline to Finish

Random Thoughts

Random Thoughts

Week 35

Main Goal For This Week

Steps I Can Take to Reach It

171.

172.

173.

174.

175.

Reward if I Make Good Progress

Obstacles I May Face	How I Will Deal With Them

Accountability Partner

Deadline to Finish

Random Thoughts

Random Thoughts

Week 36

Main Goal For This Week

Steps I Can Take to Reach It

176.

177.

178.

179.

180.

Reward if I Make Good Progress

Obstacles I May Face	How I Will Deal With Them

Accountability Partner

Deadline to Finish

Random Thoughts

Random Thoughts

Week 37

Main Goal For This Week

_____

_____

_____

_____

Steps I Can Take to Reach It

181.

182.

183.

184.

185.

Reward if I Make Good Progress

_____

_____

Obstacles I May Face	How I Will Deal With Them

Accountability Partner

Deadline to Finish

Random Thoughts

Random Thoughts

Week 38

Main Goal For This Week

Steps I Can Take to Reach It

186.

187.

188.

189.

190.

Reward if I Make Good Progress

Obstacles I May Face	How I Will Deal With Them

Accountability Partner

_____

_____

Deadline to Finish

_____

_____

Random Thoughts

Random Thoughts

Week 39

Main Goal For This Week

Steps I Can Take to Reach It

191.

192.

193.

194.

195.

Reward if I Make Good Progress

Obstacles I May Face	How I Will Deal With Them

Accountability Partner

Deadline to Finish

Random Thoughts

Random Thoughts

Week 40

Main Goal For This Week

Steps I Can Take to Reach It

196.

197.

198.

199.

200.

Reward if I Make Good Progress

Obstacles I May Face	How I Will Deal With Them

Accountability Partner

Deadline to Finish

Random Thoughts

Random Thoughts

Week 41

Main Goal For This Week

_____

_____

_____

_____

Steps I Can Take to Reach It

201.

202.

203.

204.

205.

Reward if I Make Good Progress

_____

_____

Obstacles I May Face	How I Will Deal With Them

Accountability Partner

Deadline to Finish

Random Thoughts

Random Thoughts

Week 42

Main Goal For This Week

Steps I Can Take to Reach It

206.

207.

208.

209.

210.

Reward if I Make Good Progress

Obstacles I May Face	How I Will Deal With Them

Accountability Partner

Deadline to Finish

Random Thoughts

Random Thoughts

Week 43

Main Goal For This Week

Steps I Can Take to Reach It

211.

212.

213.

214.

215.

Reward if I Make Good Progress

Obstacles I May Face	How I Will Deal With Them

Accountability Partner

Deadline to Finish

Random Thoughts

Random Thoughts

Week 44

Main Goal For This Week

Steps I Can Take to Reach It

216.

217.

218.

219.

220.

Reward if I Make Good Progress

Obstacles I May Face	How I Will Deal With Them

Accountability Partner

Deadline to Finish

Random Thoughts

Random Thoughts

Week 45

Main Goal For This Week

Steps I Can Take to Reach It

221.

222.

223.

224.

225.

Reward if I Make Good Progress

Obstacles I May Face	How I Will Deal With Them

Accountability Partner

Deadline to Finish

Random Thoughts

Random Thoughts

Week 46

Main Goal For This Week

_____

_____

_____

_____

Steps I Can Take to Reach It

226.

227.

228.

229.

230.

Reward if I Make Good Progress

_____

_____

Obstacles I May Face	How I Will Deal With Them

Accountability Partner

Deadline to Finish

Random Thoughts

Random Thoughts

Week 47

Main Goal For This Week

_____

_____

_____

_____

Steps I Can Take to Reach It

231.

232.

233.

234.

235.

Reward if I Make Good Progress

_____

_____

Obstacles I May Face	How I Will Deal With Them

Accountability Partner

Deadline to Finish

Random Thoughts

Random Thoughts

Week 48

Main Goal For This Week

Steps I Can Take to Reach It

236.

237.

238.

239.

240.

Reward if I Make Good Progress

Obstacles I May Face	How I Will Deal With Them

Accountability Partner

Deadline to Finish

Random Thoughts

Random Thoughts

Week 49

Main Goal For This Week

Steps I Can Take to Reach It

241.

242.

243.

244.

245.

Reward if I Make Good Progress

Obstacles I May Face	How I Will Deal With Them

Accountability Partner

Deadline to Finish

Random Thoughts

Random Thoughts

Week 50

Main Goal For This Week

_____

_____

_____

_____

Steps I Can Take to Reach It

246.

247.

248.

249.

250.

Reward if I Make Good Progress

_____

_____

Obstacles I May Face	How I Will Deal With Them

Accountability Partner

Deadline to Finish

Random Thoughts

Random Thoughts

Week 51

Main Goal For This Week

_____

_____

_____

_____

Steps I Can Take to Reach It

251.

252.

253.

254.

255.

Reward if I Make Good Progress

_____

_____

Obstacles I May Face	How I Will Deal With Them

Accountability Partner

Deadline to Finish

Random Thoughts

Random Thoughts

Week 52

Main Goal For This Week

Steps I Can Take to Reach It

256.

257.

258.

259.

260.

Reward if I Make Good Progress

Obstacles I May Face	How I Will Deal With Them

Accountability Partner

Deadline to Finish

Random Thoughts

Random Thoughts

Thank you for investing your time and energy into your goals this year.

I hope this workbook has helped you step boldly closer to your dreams coming true.

Even though you've come to the end of this workbook, your goal travels still continue.

Keep at it and you will succeed.

Blessings to you always.

Rev. Bill McBride

S.M.A.R.T. GOALS MIND MAP

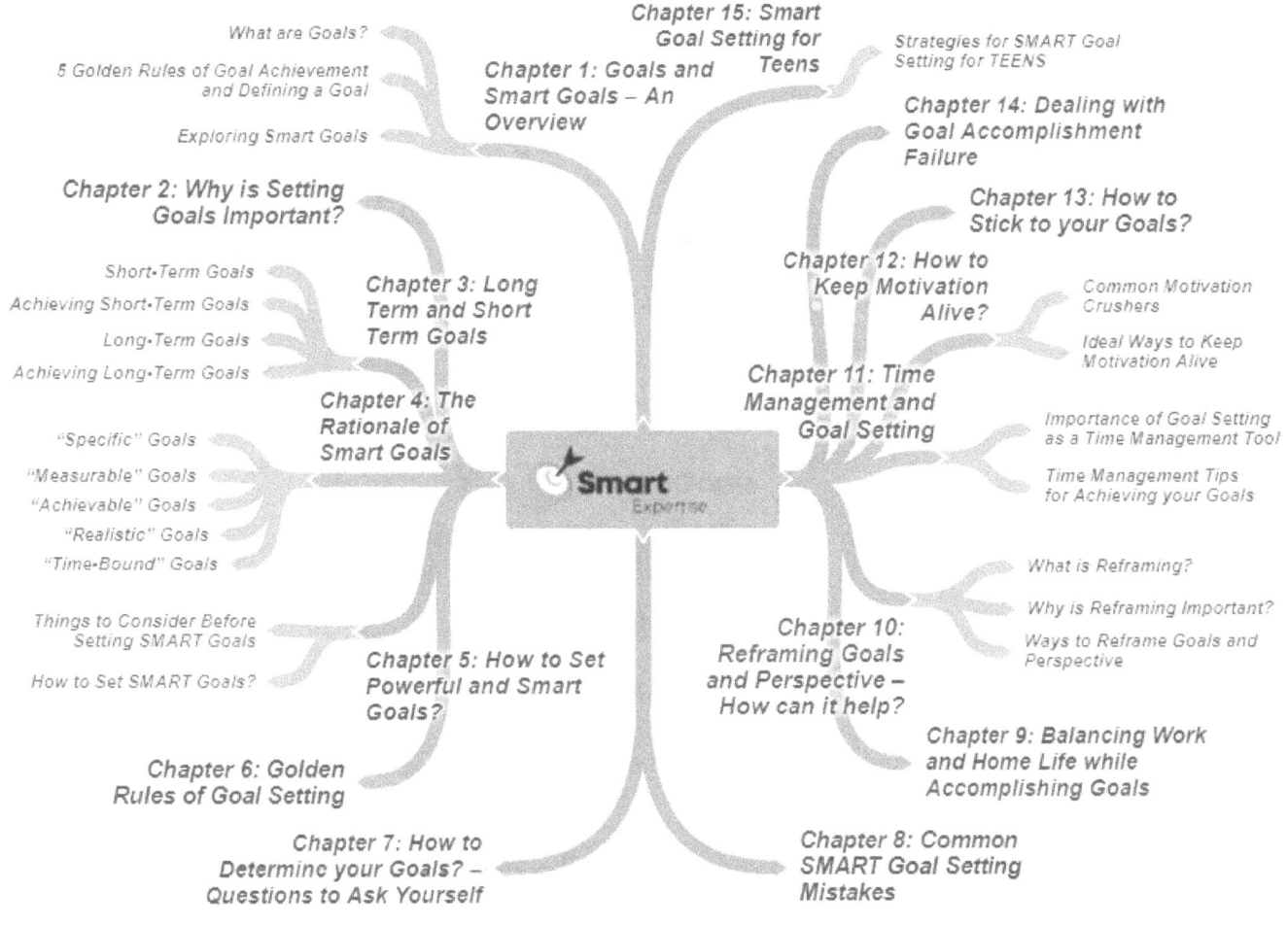

What are Goals?

5 Golden Rules of Goal Achievement and Defining a Goal

Exploring Smart Goals

Chapter 1: Goals and Smart Goals – An Overview

Chapter 15: Smart Goal Setting for Teens

Strategies for SMART Goal Setting for TEENS

Chapter 14: Dealing with Goal Accomplishment Failure

Chapter 2: Why is Setting Goals Important?

Chapter 13: How to Stick to your Goals?

Short-Term Goals

Achieving Short-Term Goals

Long-Term Goals

Achieving Long-Term Goals

Chapter 3: Long Term and Short Term Goals

Chapter 12: How to Keep Motivation Alive?

Common Motivation Crushers

Ideal Ways to Keep Motivation Alive

Chapter 4: The Rationale of Smart Goals

Chapter 11: Time Management and Goal Setting

Importance of Goal Setting as a Time Management Tool

Time Management Tips for Achieving your Goals

"Specific" Goals

"Measurable" Goals

"Achievable" Goals

"Realistic" Goals

"Time-Bound" Goals

Smart Expertise

What is Reframing?

Why is Reframing Important?

Ways to Reframe Goals and Perspective

Things to Consider Before Setting SMART Goals

How to Set SMART Goals?

Chapter 5: How to Set Powerful and Smart Goals?

Chapter 10: Reframing Goals and Perspective – How can it help?

Chapter 9: Balancing Work and Home Life while Accomplishing Goals

Chapter 6: Golden Rules of Goal Setting

Chapter 7: How to Determine your Goals? – Questions to Ask Yourself

Chapter 8: Common SMART Goal Setting Mistakes

https://YourSpiritualityMatters.com/Goals

This mind map is a preview of the FREE Training Guide available on the Goals Resource & Training page.

Join the Goal Achievers Community and get your **FREE goal training and resources**.

Go here to sign up:
https://YourSpiritualityMatters.com/Goals